Rules for Success

Time-Tested Keys for Developing Excellence in Your Life

Mamie McCul

RIVER
OAK
PUBLISHING

Tulsa, Oklahoma

Rules for Success
Time-Tested Keys for Developing Excellence in Your Life
ISBN 1-58919-012-X
Copyright © 2002 by Mamie McCullough
PMB 372
305 Spring Creek Village
Dallas, Texas 75248

06 05 04 03 02   10 9 8 7 6 5 4

Published by RiverOak Publishing
P. O. Box 700143
Tulsa, Oklahoma 74170-0143

Introduction

Success! All people seek it. To some people it means money, power, and fame. To others it means family, peace, and contentment. Whatever your definition of success, the rules for reaching any goal are remarkably similar. The most important of these are here for you. Success rarely occurs accidentally, but almost always results when desire and knowledge are put into action.

Your dreams can come true. They can! No matter where you start or what has happened to you. YOU CAN BE A WINNER IN LIFE! You can reach any goal you choose and get there quicker and easier when you know what to do in various situations. The ideas in this book are proven and have helped me and countless others over a long period of time. My experience is that one good idea can change your life for the better! Together these rules form a powerful strategy, giving you that extra edge everyone needs to be successful.

I BELIEVE IN YOU!

Mamie McCullough

THE KEY DECISION... START NOW!

The way to get ahead is to start now. If you start now, you will know a lot next year that you don't know now and that you would not have known next year if you had waited.

— WILLIAM FEATHER

GET READY... OPPORTUNITY AHEAD

A*ny age is the right age to start doing.*

— **GERARD**

There are exciting opportunities ahead, regardless of your situation today. To be successful, we must get ready and take full advantage of them when they come our way. Analyze your previous responses and start fixing anything that prevents you from capitalizing on a new situation. Rid yourself of whatever might limit your ability to recognize and fully benefit from each new opportunity. Success is closer and more certain when you use today to — get ready!

ALL IT TAKES...JUST DO YOUR BEST TODAY

The past, the present, and the future are really one...they are today.

— STOWE

Looks, IQ, or size do not matter...Just Do Your Best Today.

The past does not count...Just Do Your Best Today.

You will learn as you go...Just Do Your Best Today.

All success starts small...Just Do Your Best Today.

Others will help you on your way...Just Do Your Best Today.

Your best will get better...Just Do Your Best Today.

Your dreams start coming true when you...Just Do Your Best Today.

OTHERS WILL HELP YOU SUCCEED

We cannot hold a torch to light another's path without brightening our own.

— BEN SWEETLAND

Many will help as you try to succeed. Some will not. Sometimes the ones you would expect to help either cannot or will not. Don't worry...there will be others who can and will. Successful people are almost always willing to help someone else succeed. Watch and learn how they handle the situations that cause you difficulty. Ask for specific advice, but respect their time restraints. You are not alone! Others will help you along the road to success.

LIFE IS A WHOLE SEASON... NOT ONE GAME

Keep true, never be ashamed of doing right; decide on what you think is right, and stick to it.

— **GEORGE ELIOT**

We can be very successful despite the fact we are destined to lose some games in life's season. The best professional football team will lose about three games before winning the Super Bowl. The best professional basketball team will taste defeat about twenty times. The World Series baseball champions will lose over fifty times. These teams are the best...even though they lose a few games. You can be like them. Be prepared, play hard, and play every game to win. Learn from the inevitable losses and go on to a successful life season.

REPLACE ALL NEGATIVES WITH POSITIVES

Sun is delicious, rain is refreshing, wind braces up, snow is exhilarating; there is no such thing as bad weather, only different kinds of good weather.

— **RUSKIN**

Most of us understand the importance of eliminating negatives from our lives and replacing them with positives. The best way I know of doing this is by using what is called the "Replacement Theory." You force out negatives of all types by putting positives in and leaving no room for negatives. By filling your mind with positive thoughts, books, ideas, foods, people, etc., negatives are automatically eliminated, because all available space is taken by positives.

CONCENTRATE ON SMALL IMPROVEMENTS

When we have done our best...we can await the result in peace.

— J. LUBBOCK

You would like to have a positive impact on your world and do something worthwhile and important in your chosen field. Great! The desire to do well is always the first step, and concentrating on small improvements is the easiest and most effective way to make a difference. Major accomplishments result when we consistently make many small improvements over a period of time. Every small improvement makes things better and brings you a step closer to the major success you desire.

MAKE PLEASANT MEMORIES ALONG THE WAY

A *sense of humor is the oil of life's engine. Without it, the machinery creaks and groans. No lot is so hard, no aspect of things so grim, but it relaxes before a hearty laugh.*

— **G. S. MERRIAM**

Success is hollow without pleasant memories along the way. When you recall them, they bring a smile to your face and a bounce in your step. These are needed for real success. The best memories are made with other people and cost very little. Take time with those you care about to do something, go somewhere, and have fun! It enhances any journey when you laugh and enjoy each other along the way.

You Can't Make A Good Deal With A Bad Person

Fool me once, shame on you;

fool me twice, shame on me.

— **Chinese Proverb**

I am convinced that we should be pleasant, supportive, and encouraging to everyone we meet. It is equally important, however, to only deal with reliable, reputable people when significant emotional energy or money is involved. Make important alliances with trustworthy people. Tremendous financial and emotional capital can be lost if you deal with those of questionable reputation. This applies to any important relationship.

MOST WINS ARE BY SMALL MARGINS

The person who wins may have been counted out several times, but did not hear the referee.

— H. E. JANSEN

In everything you do, give a little extra effort. Often there is very little difference between a win and a loss. That is not only true in sports, but also in the more important game of life. There is often a very small margin between success and failure. As you consistently apply that something extra, it will result in wins that will surprise both you and your opposition. Try harder and win the close ones.

LUCK HAS VERY LITTLE TO DO WITH SUCCESS

I had six honest serving men —

they taught me all I knew.

Their names were Where and

What and When — and Why

and How and Who.

— RUDYARD KIPLING

Successful people do not think much about luck. They certainly do not depend on it. Of course, they gladly accept the little extra push it gives when it comes their way. However, they realize that luck visits everyone on an unpredictable schedule, and persistent effort, wise choices, and intelligent planning are better horses to ride in any quest for success.

MANY OPPORTUNITIES COME FROM NEW FRIENDS

Small opportunities are often the beginning of great enterprises.

— **DEMOSTHENES**

Success comes quickly when you expand your circle to include new, quality people. These are people who can teach you, challenge you, and encourage you. Old friends and business associates can be wonderful, but your circle of associates must constantly expand if you are to reach your full potential. My belief is that many of your new, important opportunities come from new friends or associates. Searching out these quality people gives you the best possible chance for progress toward your goals.

Do Not Share Everything With Others

The secret of being tiresome is to tell everything.

— Voltaire

Many things should be shared with others. Share your enthusiasm, your ideas, your encouragement, your lunch, or anything else that will help them. But never share your "nitty-gritty." These are your irritations, aches, pains, complaints, or anything else no one wants to hear. The fact that you do not share unnecessary and mundane things will be appreciated, and you will be welcome in any company.

DO NOT WATCH THE NEWS... MAKE THE NEWS

Have confidence that if you have done a little thing well, you can do a bigger thing well, too.

— STOREY

Hopefully you do not spend too much time watching the news on television or reading the newspaper. It is important to stay informed, but many people consume too much fluff. Let's continue to use our energies to accomplish worthwhile goals — things that some day may make the news! The world awaits your contribution, and one of the keys is to *watch* less and *do* more.

LEARN LIFE'S DANGEROUS LESSONS FROM OTHERS

The world is full of cactus,

but we don't have to sit on it.

— **WILL FOLEY**

Eventually, each of us will learn most of life's dangerous lessons. Success comes easier and with fewer bumps and bruises when we learn from the experiences of others. Be alert. Watch others. Notice how drugs, alcohol, fast driving, and the wrong kind of friends bring trouble or even kill. Learn the fun lessons for yourself, but the dangerous ones from others.

**POSITIVE
ACTION
ALWAYS
BRINGS
POSITIVE
RESULTS**

"I *Cannot Do It*" *never*

accomplished anything. "*I Will*

Try" *has performed wonders.*

— **GEORGE BUNHEM**

Be confident that taking positive action as often as possible will result in rewards. Positive results may be delayed, but ultimately, they will always occur. You will enjoy the results of taking positive action. It is similar to investing in a "sure thing." You will get much more out of it than you put in, and you will be investing in something near and dear — yourself.

ALL MAJOR SUCCESS IS A JOINT EFFORT

The Constitution only guarantees pursuit of happiness...you have to catch up with it yourself.

— GILL ROBB WILSON

Your associations with other people will go a long way in determining the timing and extent of your success. Carefully choose the people who will assist you and work with you in your endeavors. All major success is the result of people coming together for a common purpose. Your success will be faster and easier if you carefully assemble and nurture your team. Most successful individuals have help behind the scenes.

GENEROSITY IS BOTH RIGHT AND REWARDING

A *man there was, they called him mad...the more he gave, the more he had.*

— **BUNYON**

Generous people are almost always more successful than those who greedily hold on to everything that comes within their grasp. Practice generosity whether you have a little or a lot. Start by being generous with honest compliments and encouragement. Give good advice and recognition, and then add tangible forms of generosity as circumstances permit. Do what you can, when you can, wherever you can, to share your blessings with others.

LIFE PICKS ON EVERYONE... DO NOT TAKE IT PERSONALLY

People are not against you;

they are merely for themselves.

— GENE FOWLER

You will avoid wasting a great deal of emotional energy if you do not take life's bumps and bruises personally. People will pick on you and cause you grief in many ways. You may not deserve it, but it is inevitable. When you think it is directed at you alone, it hurts more. Therefore, it is vital to understand those same people give everyone grief! It is much easier to move on when you remember it's not personal. Emotional energy is extremely valuable and should be saved to expend on important projects.

Be World-class... Strive For Quality

The great at anything do not set to work because they are inspired, but rather become inspired because they are working. They don't waste time waiting for inspiration.

— Ernest Newman

A world-class person is one who is capable of competing at the highest level in some area of expertise. Strive for quality in every area of your life. The happiest and most successful people are always striving to be better. They are constantly on the lookout for ways to improve. I am convinced each of us has the ability to be world-class in some area. Find your niche, strive for quality, and become one of those who is truly "world-class."

Don't Count On Changing Other People

Lost...somewhere between sunrise and sunset, sixty golden minutes. Each set with sixty diamond seconds. No reward is offered, for they are gone forever.

— Horace Mann

Would you like to know how your friends or associates will react to a particular situation? In all probability, they will react exactly like they did the last time they were faced with the same conditions. Most people do. The lesson here is: Do not make major plans based on someone else changing. Do not risk your future on the hope you can change someone. Encouraging positive change is admirable, but wait to see the fruit of change before making plans.

RETAIN OR REGAIN YOUR INTEGRITY

There can be no such thing as a necessary evil. For if a thing is really necessary, it cannot be an evil and if it is an evil, it is not necessary.

— **TIORIO**

Without integrity we may experience minor success, but we will never be a complete success. My definition of integrity is the agreement of our actions with our core beliefs. Any struggle necessary to maintain or regain your integrity is worthwhile. Integrity makes all progress easier. Regain your integrity if you have temporarily compromised it. Integrity will return when you choose once again to base all your decisions and actions on your moral beliefs.

GET WHAT YOU WANT BY A-S-K-I-N-G

There are more goods bought by the heart than by the head.

— GEORGE HENNING

You don't g-e-t until you a-s-k. For years this rule has been the number one way to get what you need or want. History shows that many great things have been accomplished by ordinary people. They succeeded because they asked others to join them. People cannot read your mind. If someone has the ability to meet your need, just ask. Always make it a win/win situation by providing something of value to them in return. This rule applies across the whole spectrum of relationships.

LIFE IS OFTEN UNFAIR, SUCCEED ANYWAY

God does not want us to do extraordinary things. He wants us to do ordinary things extraordinarily well.

— **BISHOP GORE**

It has been said there are many reasons for failure, but no excuse for it. This statement has an important point. You may not deserve the bad things that have or will happen to you, but you can and must overcome them and go on to achieve success. Keep your eye on the goal ahead and ignore any unfairness that comes your way. Today's most successful people have had to face and overcome many of the same obstacles. You can too!

SPOIL YOUR EMPLOYERS WHETHER THEY DESERVE IT OR NOT

Action may not always bring happiness...but there is no happiness without action.

— BENJAMIN DISRAELI

The majority of us will work for someone else most of our lives. Decide now to be the best employee they will ever have. Spoil them with your performance. Some will not deserve your dedication, but do it anyway. It's really for your benefit, because there is no faster way to promotion. People around you will notice and the word will spread, even to other potential employers. They will advance you if your current employer is unwilling.

All Good Things Start Small

Here is a simple, but powerful rule...always give people more than they expect to get.

— Nelson Boswell

A few years ago in a tiny office out in the desert, two young men started what is now the world's largest computer software company. That company is Microsoft, and the two young men are now billionaires Bill Gates and Paul Allen. All success, whether in business or personal, starts small. You can do the same, even late in life. Ray Kroc was in his fifties when he opened a place called McDonald's. Start small and watch your business grow big!

ALL DECISIONS ARE NOT EQUAL

In matters of conscience, first thoughts are best. In matters of prudence, last thoughts are best.

— ROBERT HALL

Experts disagree about the speed with which decisions should be made. Some believe quick decisions are best, while others believe things should be thought through slowly and deliberately. However, experts do agree that all decisions are not equal. It does not really matter where you eat lunch, but who you choose as a life or business partner is vital to your success. Spend little time on decisions that have little impact in the long run, but take as long as necessary with the important ones.

START FROM WHERE YOU ARE NOW

It's so hard when I have to....

And so easy when I want to.

— **SONDRA ANICE BARNES**

It is almost magical how much distance you can cover in one day on our interstate highways. We drive about sixty thousand miles a year, besides all the air travel. We have learned you can start from any place with a good map and go anywhere you want. The same is true with success. With a good map, you can start where you are now and reach your goals. No matter where you are, start now and you can go wherever you want to go.

SOME DECISIONS ARE BEST MADE ONLY ONCE

We must make automatic and habitual, as early as possible, as many actions as we can. The more of the daily details of life we can hand over to the effortless custody of automatism, the more our higher powers of mind can be set free for their own proper work.

— WILLIAM JAMES

Make important decisions only once and escape the necessity of rehashing them again and again. These are usually decisions on how we are going to live. For example, we will decide to be honest, to be on time, and to go to church on Sunday. We make commitments carefully, then keep them. Make these types of decisions only once. It will clear your mind of unnecessary clutter and take you on to a better way of life.

You Do Not Have To Feel Good To Do Good

We are not here to play,

to dream, to drift.

We have hard work to do

and loads to lift.

Shun not the struggle —

face it, 'tis God's gift.

— **Shaftesbury**

It is exciting when you come to the understanding that you can and will do some of your best work when you don't feel like working. How you feel when you start has only a marginal impact on the quality of your output. People who wait to do things until they feel like it are doomed to mediocrity or worse. Great things can be accomplished when you are beset by aches and pains, either physical or emotional. Do good now, regardless, then you will feel better later.

IMPROVE YOUR SPEECHES AND PRESENTATIONS

It usually takes a little more than three weeks to prepare a good impromptu speech.

— **MARK TWAIN [IN JEST]**

The key to dramatically better speeches and presentations is focus. The most common problem: Being too focused on yourself, and what the result of your presentation will be for you. Will the audience like you? Will they buy? Instead, focus on what you can give to or share with your audience. Focus on what you can do for them, and forget about what may or may not happen to you. You will make the most effective presentations when you focus on the audience's needs and forget your own.

BE AN EXPERT IN YOUR FIELD

Talent alone won't make you a success. Neither will being in the right place at the right time, unless you are ready. The most important question is always: "Are you ready?"

— JOHNNY CARSON

Good or bad, we are living in a period of specialization. Whatever your area of interest, decide to become as knowledgeable as possible. It is important, perhaps vital, to your future. Experts are always able to command a premium for their services and usually enjoy prestige and other benefits. The time and effort invested are well worth it as you become an expert in your chosen field.

PRACTICE MAKES YOU GOOD... MAYBE EVEN GREAT

Have patience. All things are difficult before they become easy.

— SAADI

Do you want to be really good at whatever you choose to do? Among the handful of necessary ingredients, practice may be the most important part of achieving this goal. People constantly ask me how they can become a professional speaker. My answer is to make as many speeches as possible to any group who will listen. This applies to any activity. Repetition is the key to improvement. Practice still makes perfect. To do anything well — practice, practice, practice.

LISTEN MORE... LEARN MORE... MOVE UP FASTER

True wisdom lies in gathering the precious things out of each day as it goes by.

— E. S. BOUTON

We should all listen more and listen better. Be aware of the absolute fact that we learn nothing new while we are talking. In conversation we only learn new things when someone else is talking. Listen more and learn more. It is also important to understand we can learn something from everyone. Useful ideas often come from unexpected sources, and often from unimpressive people.

Give More Value In Whatever You Do

The fact is, nothing comes; at least nothing good. All has to be fetched.

— **Charles Buxton**

"**G**ive More Value" is an appropriate motto for these times. More value may be the defining difference between success and failure. To succeed, we must give more value to our services or products. More than ever purchasers are demanding increased value. Don't fight this fact, but accept it and distance yourself ahead of your competition. Work smarter, harder, and more creatively to provide the best value in whatever you do.

You Can Start Over And Still Win Big

The gem cannot be polished without friction...nor you perfected without trials.

— **Chinese Proverb**

My hope is that all is well with you and your life is on a steady, upward path. However, if you experience a devastating loss of some kind, it is important to know you can start over and still win big. The Dallas Cowboys football team won only one game in 1989, but became the Super Bowl champions in 1992, 1993, and 1995. Lee Iacocca was fired as president of Ford before reviving both his own career and Chrysler Corporation. Oprah Winfrey was fired in Cincinnati before moving to Chicago. Win big...even if you must start over.

CALL YOUR TROUBLES EXPERIENCES OR CHALLENGES

A *laugh is worth one hundred groans in any market.*

— LAMB

May I encourage you to avoid using the word "troubles"? Just take it out of your vocabulary. Replace it with phrases like "interesting experiences," "unusual experiences," or "exciting challenges." Use these and soon you will come to understand that a life of experiences and challenges is a much more pleasant one. Whatever the name, these events are better solved by people with a positive approach. Get rid of the "T" word.

SMALL CHANGES MAY MAKE YOU A CREATIVE GENIUS

I never did a day's work in my life. It was all fun!

— THOMAS A. EDISON

Creativity is highly desired and often richly rewarded. Those who are not creative like to associate with those who are. Most people who are considered creative simply began making small modifications to existing ideas. They changed a few words, a few physical characteristics of a product, or added a new aspect to an old plan. Uniquely paint the wheel, and you are as creative as the inventor of the wheel. Make small, innovative changes to the existing order to become creative.

You Just Need A Tune-Up... Not An Overhaul

God gives every bird its food...

but he does not throw it into

the nest.

— J. G. HOLLAND

The most sophisticated computer is completely disabled if a couple of connections are loose. Does the device then need to be replaced or completely overhauled? No! All we need to do is to tighten the connections, a very minor repair. The same is true when we are not operating properly. We may feel totally messed up and in need of a major overhaul. But in most cases, all we need is a few minor adjustments for our original power and performance to return. Find and fix these minor problems.

WORK IS A BLESSING... NOT A CURSE

There is no easy method of accomplishing difficult things. The method is to close the door, tell people you are not at home...and work.

— **JOSEPH DE MAISTRE**

We often feel hard work is a curse to be endured. Nothing could be farther from reality! The truth is: Work is a blessing! Work is often an antidote for whatever ails us. It is one of the best medicines for the multitude of maladies that attack mankind. Know that hard work is a precious gift that enhances your well-being. Be thankful if you have useful work to do. It is a blessing above all others.

SUCCEED FOR OTHERS IF NOT FOR YOURSELF

Always do right. This will gratify some and astonish the rest.

— **MARK TWAIN**

There are significant others in your life who need you to succeed. Win, and you will be better able to assist them. They can be family members or someone you love who may need your help now or later. Sometimes we almost refuse to succeed for ourselves. We feel unworthy, uninterested, or apathetic. When this is the case, succeed for someone you love. Not only will you meet their needs, but you will meet your own as well.

Call Or Write... Staying In Touch Is Important

A *determined soul will do more with a rusty wrench than others will accomplish with all the tools of a machine shop.*

— Rupert Hughes

It costs very little to call and usually even less to write some-one a short note. All successful people usually stay in close contact with friends and business associates. Some are almost fanatical in this regard. It is smart to stay in touch. Most opportunity comes from other people. Share information, ideas, and encouragement. One of the best investments in your future is to stay in touch.

ACCOMPLISHMENT IS THE KEY TO HAPPINESS

Money never starts an idea; it is the idea that starts the money.

— W. J. CAMERON

One of the deepest needs of our soul is to accomplish something worthwhile. We need to reach goals, win victories, and taste success. Recreation, rest, and various kinds of entertainment have their place, but accomplishment nurtures the spirit. An interesting fact is that we get about the same lift from small accomplishments as from big ones. Small victories are often the most fulfilling. Win big or win small — but reaching a few goals will make you happier!

JOIN THE MOST SUCCESSFUL PEOPLE IN TOWN

Always vote for principle, although you vote alone, and you may cherish the sweet reflection that your vote is never lost.

— JOHN QUINCY ADAMS

Associate with winners and some of their winning ways will rub off on you. Be around losers too long and your prospects are severely limited. Where do you find the happiest, most successful, highest achievers? You may find them anywhere, but my experience tells me they are most likely found in the churches of your community. Join them there for another more important reason, but just being around them will help in your quest for success.

HIGH ENERGY IS A NECESSARY INGREDIENT FOR SUCCESS

If you care strongly enough for a result...you will almost certainly attain it.

— **WILLIAM JAMES**

High energy is almost always present in successful people. There is a correlation between energy level and success level. Among other positive results, high energy permits you to hold your course to success when things get tough. My best idea for increasing energy is to eat more fruits and veggies, eat less fat, and get on a reasonable program of exercise. This is also the conclusion of most valid books on the subject. Start now!

SUCCESS IS ALMOST ALWAYS PRECEDED BY ADVERSITY

Successful people have learned to make themselves do the thing that has to be done when it has to be done, whether they like it or not.

— ALDUS HUXLEY

Study the history of any successful organization, business, or individual and you will almost always find their success was preceded by a period of difficulty and even disaster. Progress is neither uniform nor guaranteed, but let me urge you: Fight through your difficult periods, regardless of their nature or extent. Realize they are often necessary to prepare you for your biggest triumphs which lie ahead. The great times are often found just past adversity.

EVERYONE NEEDS RULES AND LIMITS

There is a foolish corner in the

brain of the wisest person.

— **ARISTOTLE**

Young or old, employee or employer, whatever your status, we all need rules and limits within which to live and pursue our goals. Operating within boundaries of integrity and safety enables us to reach our full potential. For example, if there were not rules of the road we could not travel in relative safety to distant places. Some rules are provided for us, while in many areas we are free to choose our own. Valid rules and limits are essential to our well-being and success.

WEEDS ARE PART OF LIFE

Big shots are only little shots

who keep shooting.

— **CHRISTOPHER MORLEY**

Personal weeds are blemishes in the garden of your life. They are false steps, irritations, and problems. While they may start small, they often cause serious damage, if not dealt with early. They are inevitable and can never be totally avoided. Like real weeds, they are best handled as soon as their appearance is noticed, before their roots are well established. Make it your policy to immediately eliminate life's weeds as they appear.

DECIDE WHAT YOU WANT AND PAY THE PRICE

The person who will use his skill and constructive imagination to see how much he can give for a dollar, instead of how much he can get for a dollar, is bound to succeed.

— HENRY FORD

Everything has a price — both tangible and intangible things. In some cases the price is paid by someone else, but in most cases it must be paid by you. Effort, energy, money, and time are the most common forms of payment. Therefore, after you decide what you want, carefully consider the full price and what it is worth to you. If the result is positive, pay the price, whatever it may be, and enjoy!

USE THE MOST IMPORTANT CARD YOU HAVE

Today a Reader...tomorrow a Leader.

— W. FUSSELMAN

The most important card you have is not your MasterCard, your Visa, your American Express, or your Discover. My belief is that the most important card you own is your library card. If you don't have one, get one. It can provide you with valuable information, motivation, recreation, and much more. It costs practically nothing, and the atmosphere is always quiet and pleasant. Use and support your local library. It is one of the few truly magical places available to all.

DO MORE THAN IS NECESSARY... BUT AVOID OVERKILL

To avoid criticism...do nothing, say nothing, be nothing.

— **ELBERT HUBBARD**

To succeed at anything, it is important to do the best job you possibly can on each task. At some point, however, you can reach what I call overkill. This is the point where additional effort would be better spent on the next project. Additional effort on the initial task does not provide a better result, but merely uses valuable resources best used elsewhere. This is a judgment call, but you will make a better decision when you realize there is a maximum effort point beyond which is wasted overkill.

BRAINSTORM ...SOMEONE ALREADY HAS THE ANSWER

Experience shows that success is due less to ability than to zeal. The winner is the one that gives all to the quest, body and soul.

— **CHARLES BUXTON**

Please be assured, someone has the answer to that perplexing situation you are facing. The way to solve most problems when you don't have the answer is to discuss them with competent friends or associates. Throw a wide net if the problem is difficult, getting the largest possible group to brainstorm the solution. In the past, these sessions were usually done in a group meeting. Today, many are done by phone.

Fix The Problem... Not The Blame

Either I will find a way, or I will make one.

— P. Sidney

There will always be an oversupply of people who spend a large portion of their time figuring out who to blame when things go wrong. However, the real demand is for people who fix the problem, not the blame. Even if you know who is to blame, rather than talking about blame, talk about solutions to the problem. Those who concentrate on fixing problems are paid well, while blame fixers are lucky to hang on to their jobs. Problem fixers are always needed and welcome.

PLANT IN FERTILE SOIL

Opportunity rarely knocks until you are ready. And few people have been really ready without receiving opportunity's call.

— CHANNING POLLOCK

Opportunity is greater and success is more sure if you pick the right area in which to pursue your dreams. For example, look for areas of fast growth to find the best job opportunities. At times we have little choice but to do the best we can, where we are, in what we are doing. But eventually we do have choices. Then we need to focus on the newer, faster growing enterprises. Try to cast your lot with quality growth opportunities. Everyone moves up faster in these situations.

Avoid Excess That Dulls The Mind

All that I have seen teaches me to trust the Creator for all I have not seen.

— **Ralph Waldo Emerson**

Success is largely found in sharp, vibrant, alert, with-it type people. To be among those types we must avoid anything that dulls our mind or body. The obvious are alcohol and drugs. The less obvious are those things that are good and beneficial in moderation, but energy-sapping when used in excess. This category includes food, television, video games, internet surfing, and many others. Increase your chances for success by moderating these activities.

TOMORROW IS PAY DAY FOR WHAT YOU DO TODAY

God does not charge time spent helping others against a person's allotted life span.

— **AMERICAN INDIAN PROVERB**

We all have come to understand and accept the principle of work first and get paid later. In all types of business relationships, this principle applies. It also applies to almost every other area of life. We are rewarded in the future for our efforts today. Want to have a great future? Then have a great today. The effort we put forth today will result in more satisfying — and profitable — tomorrows.

**PROBLEMS
BECOME
SMALLER
WHEN YOU
DON'T
DODGE
THEM**

Do what you know best;

if you are a runner, run,

if you're a bell, ring.

— **IGNAS BERNSTEIN**

This next idea is so vital I hope you give it extra consideration. The most important step you can take to shrink or eliminate any problem is to face it, analyze it, and start taking action to solve it. Difficulties rarely go away without effective action. All major problems usually started small and grew as they were ignored. Much less energy and effort are needed when they are caught and handled early. You take a quantum leap toward success when you attack problems immediately.

A GOOD STRATEGY GETS YOU TO SUCCESS QUICKER

A *good plan is like a road map...it shows the final destination and usually marks the best way to get there.*

— H. STANLEY JUDD

Strategy is defined as the plan used to reach a specific goal. With a good plan, you are guided directly toward your goal with the least amount of wasted effort. You know you are on the best path to reach your goal, so you can concentrate on working the plan. Who should devise the strategy? Probably you, but don't hesitate to ask others for suggestions and ideas. Use the best strategy...authorship is optional.

No Second Chances... But Lots Of New Chances

Even if you are on the right track you'll get run over if you just sit there.

— WILL ROGERS

The bad news is, there are no second chances to relive the past. This fact underlines the importance of doing our best every time, because we will never again have the same opportunity under the same circumstances. The good news is, we can expect other chances and new opportunities to continue to come our way. The challenge is to take full advantage of these as they occur. Learn from the past and take full advantage of what the future brings.

DON'T WORRY ABOUT WHAT YOU CAN'T CONTROL

There is a way to do it better...

find it!

— **THOMAS A. EDISON**

All our efforts must be focused on things under our control. If we become concerned about things we cannot control, we waste energy that could have been better spent elsewhere. Successful people refuse to be overwhelmed with the fact that some things are outside their control. They know they can only be effective by applying maximum effort to those areas where they have influence. Concentrate on your decisions and your actions. Disregard whatever or whoever falls outside your control.

WATCH WHAT THEY DO... NOT WHAT THEY SAY

God lends a helping hand to the one who tries hard.

— **Aeschylus**

It is important to listen carefully to what other people say. However, if you need to make an evaluation, it is much more important to watch what they do. Their actions, over time, will either prove or disprove their words. Hopefully, all our friends and associates do what they say. Nevertheless, stay armed with this effective truth detector should the need arise.

YOU CAN HAVE ANYTHING... BUT NOT EVERYTHING YOU WANT

Formula for failure...try to please everybody.

— HERBERT SWOPE

Decide what you really want...personal or professional. You can have it if you are willing to commit the necessary resources to get it. You can actually reach several of the most important goals you desire. But having everything you want is unlikely unless you have a very short list of desires — a very, very short list. So concentrate on those items at the top of your want list. Divert effort from the bottom to the top of your list, if necessary. Reach your most important goals first.

IT IS SMART TO STUDY SUCCESS

We didn't all come over on the same ship, but we are all in the same boat.

— **BERNARD BARUCH**

We learn almost everything from someone else. If we want to be successful, it is logical to learn the secrets to success from those who have achieved success. It is fascinating and instructive to see what works for others. You have really found something of value when you find common factors in your study. Usually they are traits like hard work, energy, tenacity, and the like. Study how others succeed and you increase your chances to reach success yourself.

WHEN PRESSURED... SAY NO INSTEAD OF YES

Between two evils, choose neither...between two goods, choose both.

— TRYON EDWARDS

There will be times and situations when you are pressured to make a hurried decision. It is usually someone trying to sell you something or trying to get you to agree to some proposal which requires an immediate answer. When faced with this unwanted pressure, the best answer is always no. There may be other reasons to say no, but an outstanding one is that it is always easier and more pleasant to change no to yes than to change yes to no.

OLDER DOGS CAN LEARN NEW TRICKS

When I was a boy of fourteen, my father was so ignorant I could hardly stand to have the old man around. But when I got to be twenty-one, I was astonished at how much the old boy had learned in seven years.

— MARK TWAIN

Did you know you are never too young or too old to learn new techniques or better ways to do things? It's true! Age matters little. The winners are those of any age who are always looking for more efficient solutions to life's challenges. Another advantage is that any older dog continuing to learn new tricks starts looking more and more like a pup!

SIMPLIFY YOUR LIFE AND EVERYTHING GETS EASIER

Bad luck is, in nine cases out of ten, the result of taking pleasure first and duty second, instead of duty first and pleasure second.

— **THEODORE T. MUNGER**

Most of us unnecessarily complicate things, and therefore increase our stress level. By simplifying our life, we will live better, longer, and have more fun. The best way to simplify is to reduce numbers. Less numbers of anything are easier to deal with. Reduce the item count in the refrigerator, in your closet, on your desk...everywhere. Eliminate marginal items and marginal activities wherever you can. The result is, everything becomes easier.

CHANGE YOUR TREND FROM DOWN TO UP

Learn from the mistakes of others...you can't live long enough to make them all yourself.

— **MARTIN VANBEE**

We have all been through periods in our lives when almost nothing goes right. If we plotted the trend of our life on a chart, our endeavors went steadily down. How do we change downtrends to uptrends? The answer is simple: Do things differently. We must examine the way we are doing things and change whatever or whoever is causing the poor results. Wishful thinking will not remedy our situation. Only positive changes will put us in a new upward trend.

YOUR ACTIONS DETERMINE YOUR FUTURE

The secret of success for every person who has been successful lies in the fact that he formed the habit doing those things that failures don't like to do.

— **A. JACKSON KING**

Pure and simple, your actions determine your future. This statement is accurate, precise, and encouraging if you're taking the right actions. Your future is determined by the actions you take day after day. Your actions equal your future. Positive actions equal a positive future. Do the right thing. Do the honest thing. Do the smart thing. Word hard. Play smart. Study. Love. Help others. These types of actions taken on a consistent basis will assure a bright and promising future.

SEARCH FOR NEW AND BETTER WAYS

People don't give a hoot about who made the original whatzit ...they want to know who makes the best one.

— HOWARD NEWTON

One of the fastest ways to success is to find new and better ways of doing things of value for people. Not only do you help yourself, but in many cases your change will benefit many others. Almost all aspects of daily life can be improved and made better, more efficient, or easier. Stay alert and always be on the lookout for ways to improve the current system. It is also vital to quickly incorporate new innovations that others have found.

USE THE TOOLS YOU HAVE

Nothing happens unless first a dream.

— **CARL SANDBURG**

Use whatever abilities you have to get started on the path to success. Just do your best with what you have. Do not worry about what you do not have...concentrate on the tools you are blessed with today. Many will only work under ideal conditions...but those willing to attack the situation with what they have are destined to somehow, someday acquire better tools. You have now or will receive in due time sufficient abilities to do any job.

Cut Your Losses But Never Cut And Run

My idea of an agreeable person

is one who agrees with me.

— **Benjamin Disraeli**

You will occasionally get into a situation that requires you to cut your losses. The best procedure requires a decision going in as to how much money, energy, or time you're willing to risk. Once that amount is gone and the situation has not improved...it's automatic, you are done. It's time to look for the next opportunity. You stay long enough to give the situation time to work, but not so long that you are permanently damaged if it doesn't. Make it clear up front that you will try to save the ship, but you will not go down with it!

MAKE ALL YOUR RELATIONSHIPS WIN/WIN

If fifty million people

say a foolish thing,

it is still a foolish thing.

— ANATOLE FRANCE

Most relationships important to our success are not the kind where one side wins and the other side loses. Most relationships grow and prosper when each person gets what they need from the other. When one side gets what they need...they win. When both sides get what they need, it's win/win. The best kind of transaction, whether business or personal, is the same. Structure them all so both sides get what they need and want.

CHANGE IS INEVITABLE ...MAKE IT YOUR FRIEND

Some say opportunity knocks

only once. That is not true.

Opportunity knocks all the time,

but you have to be ready for it.

— LOUIS L'AMOUR

We are in a period of rapid change in many areas. Much of it is good. Our moral and spiritual principles remain as ever, but we should gladly accept and embrace positive changes in other areas. For example, if you refuse to work with the dramatic changes in the computer industry, you do so at your own peril. Don't fight constructive change. Get on board and, if possible, get out in front! Be the first in your group to accept and champion change.

MAKE IT EASY TO DO RIGHT... HARD TO DO WRONG

All *philosophy lies in two words...sustain and abstain.*

— **EPICTETUS**

This is often called the "Number One Rule for Leaders." In all things where you have control, make it easy for you and others to do the right thing and difficult to do the wrong thing. This thought was a revelation to me when I first heard it. Where and when possible, design your own system to implement this idea. You will take a quantum leap in leadership ability at home or in the workplace. In all things...make it easy to do right and difficult to do wrong.

Pass It On...How To Say Thanks

See everything...overlook a great deal...improve what you can.

— **Pope John XXIII**

How do we say thanks to people who have helped and encouraged us? In everyone's past, there are very special people who did what others either could not or would not. We all want to repay kindness shown us, but the fact is you can never fully repay these people. You may try, but you end up short in any attempt. There is only one way to repay the debt. You pass the kindness on to someone else who needs encouragement or a helping hand. Pass It On...that's how you say "Thanks."

COPY THE BEST TECHNIQUES OF OTHERS

Cooperation is spelled with two letters...WE.

— **GEORGE VERITY**

My best compliment to successful people is to copy the way they handle certain situations. Different people do excellent work in specific areas. Use their ideas or ways of doing things if they are better than your own. Find and learn from the best. Someone is performing well at things you have difficulty with. Copy their best techniques, and over time you will eliminate many of your own weaknesses. We all need constant improvement...the best way I know is to copy the best of others.

KEEP MOVING... SUCCESS FAVORS THE MOVERS

Whoever perseveres will be crowned.

— JOHANN GOTTFRIED VON HERDER

A few years ago a popular speaker regularly used a ten-yard walk over red hot coals to demonstrate that people could do things they previously thought impossible. Without understanding the physics involved, I am convinced that the two primary rules were to 1) move straight toward the goal, and 2) keep moving. These are also excellent rules for us to follow in our quest for success. Keep your eye on the goal and keep moving toward it. Good things happen and bad things are often avoided when we keep moving toward the goal!

About the Author

Mamie McCullough is one of the country's most popular motivational speakers and authors. She addresses thousands each year through her seminars and keynote engagements: speaking to businesses, schools, and churches. She wrote the original "I CAN" program for schools and has authored three prior books.

Mamie worked with Zig Ziglar for ten years as his Director of Education. In 1989 she founded Mamie McCullough and Associates and now shares life-changing principles that are instrumental in providing strategies, ideas, suggestions, insights, and facts on how to be the best you can be. She is an encourager, author, speaker, wife, and mother. Mamie lives in Dallas, Texas, with her husband Herschel.

OTHER TITLES BY MAMIE MCCULLOUGH INCLUDE:

I Can. You Can Too!
Get it Together and Remember Where You Put It
Mama's Rules for Livin'

To contact the author for your complimentary
copy of her newsletter, *The Encourager*, write:

Mamie McCullough
PMB 372
305 Spring Creek Village
Dallas, Texas 75248